KAYAKING

BY SARA GREEN

BELLWETHER MEDIA · MINNEAPOLIS, MN

Jump into the cockpit and take flight with Pilot books. Your journey will take you on high-energy adventures as you learn about all that is wild, weird, fascinating, and fun!

This edition first published in 2013 by Bellwether Media, Inc.

No part of this publication may be reproduced in whole or in part without written permission of the publisher. For information regarding permission, write to Bellwether Media, Inc., Attention: Permissions Department, 5357 Penn Avenue South, Minneapolis, MN 55419.

Library of Congress Cataloging-in-Publication Data

Green, Sara, 1964-
Kayaking / by Sara Green.
    p. cm. – (Pilot: outdoor adventures)
Includes bibliographical references and index.
 Summary: "Engaging images accompany information about kayaking. The combination of high-interest subject matter and narrative text is intended for students in grades 3 through 7"–Provided by publisher.
 ISBN 978-1-60014-891-0 (hardcover : alk. paper)
1. Kayaking–Juvenile literature. I. Title.
 GV784.3.G75 2013
 797.122'4-dc23
                                    2012038632

Printed in the United States of America, North Mankato, MN.

TABLE OF CONTENTS

SHOOTING THE RAPIDS

A group of kayakers stands on a riverbank and listens to the roar of the rapids. They study the **whitewater** as it rushes over rocks. This is a difficult stretch, but the kayakers are experienced and up for the challenge. They slide their kayaks into the water and climb into the **cockpits**.

Soon the kayakers are shooting through the rapids. Their excitement grows as the water jumps and sprays around them. They hear a loud rumble, and the water picks up speed. The kayakers plunge down a waterfall and tumble in the rapids below. One kayaker flips upside down in an **eddy**. The others hold their breaths. Will they need to rescue their friend? In no time, the kayaker is upright. The group continues its adventure down the river.

Kayaks are sleek, lightweight boats that glide smoothly across water. They have one or more cockpits in the **deck**. Kayakers rest their feet against foot braces below the deck. They often stretch a **spray skirt** made of rubber around the opening of the cockpit. This keeps the inside of the kayak dry.

Kayak **hulls** come in different shapes. The bottoms can be flat, rounded, or shaped like the letter V. Kayaks with flat bottoms are the most steady. Kayaks with rounded or V-shaped bottoms are easier to turn.

First Kayaks

Inuit hunters built the first kayaks at least 4,000 years ago. They stretched animal skins over frames made of wood or whale bones.

spray skirt

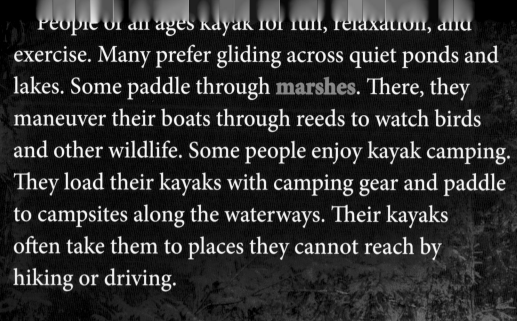

People of all ages kayak for fun, relaxation, and exercise. Many prefer gliding across quiet ponds and lakes. Some paddle through **marshes**. There, they maneuver their boats through reeds to watch birds and other wildlife. Some people enjoy kayak camping. They load their kayaks with camping gear and paddle to campsites along the waterways. Their kayaks often take them to places they cannot reach by hiking or driving.

A Record Plunge

In 2009, Tyler Bradt kayaked down Palouse Falls in Washington state. His 186-foot (57-meter) plunge earned him the world record for the highest waterfall run in a kayak.

Advanced kayakers often enjoy challenging waters. Sea kayakers paddle through open water in large lakes and along ocean shorelines. They often face strong winds and choppy waters. Many skilled kayakers participate in whitewater kayaking. Paddling through swiftly moving water can be dangerous, but it is also a thrill!

KAYAKS
AND PADDLES

Kayak designs vary to fit different uses. Sea kayaks are long and narrow. They usually measure between 14 and 19 feet (4.3 and 5.8 meters). These kayaks are designed for fast travel over long distances. They have **rudders** to help kayakers travel in straight lines through choppy water.

rudder

sea kayak

whitewater
kayak

recreational
kayak

Whitewater kayaks are shorter and wider. They are usually 6 to 8 feet (1.8 to 2.4 meters) long. Their shape makes them more stable in swift water. It also makes turning around rocks easier.

Recreational kayaks are designed for calm lakes and rivers. They are ideal for fishing, photography, and sightseeing. These kayaks are usually 9 to 14 feet (2.7 to 4.3 meters) long. Some designs allow people to sit on top of the kayak rather than in it. Many recreational kayakers appreciate the ease and comfort

Kayakers use paddles with two blades to move through the water. The blades are often spoon-shaped and **feathered** to make paddling easier. Kayakers master basic strokes. The easiest one is the forward stroke. A kayaker holds the paddle with the hands shoulder width apart. One blade enters the water near the side of the boat. Then the other blade enters the water near the other side. The rhythmic motion moves the kayaker forward.

Kayakers enjoy paddling even more when they are in good physical shape. Paddling is repetitive and involves twisting the upper body. Kayakers need **endurance** to paddle for long periods of time. Strong muscles help kayakers paddle in windy conditions and carry their kayaks with greater ease.

GEAR UP FOR FUN AND SAFETY

Kayakers should dress for the water temperature. Those paddling in cold water dress in layers of warm, lightweight clothing. The outer layer is a waterproof jacket. They also put on waterproof gloves and shoes. Many kayakers wear **dry suits** to protect themselves from cold water. Those paddling in warm water often wear swimsuits and sandals. Whitewater kayakers must also wear helmets in case they hit rocks. The helmets have ear openings that let them hear upcoming rapids and warning shouts from others. All kayakers must wear life jackets in case they flip and fall out.

Kayaks to Go

Inflatable kayaks and folding kayaks are becoming popular. These lightweight kayaks are easy to transport and store. Kayakers can even carry folding kayaks in duffel bags!

ADVENTURE ON THE WATER

Kayaking is fun, but it also has risks. Rapids can flip a kayak upside down. Kayakers must learn how to rescue themselves from the water. The Eskimo roll is one of the most common methods. After flipping over, kayakers reach their paddle toward the water's surface. Then they bump their hip against the side of the kayak. This causes the kayak to flip back into an upright position. Kayakers with spray skirts can also perform a wet exit when they are upside down. They detach their spray skirts and swim to the water's surface.

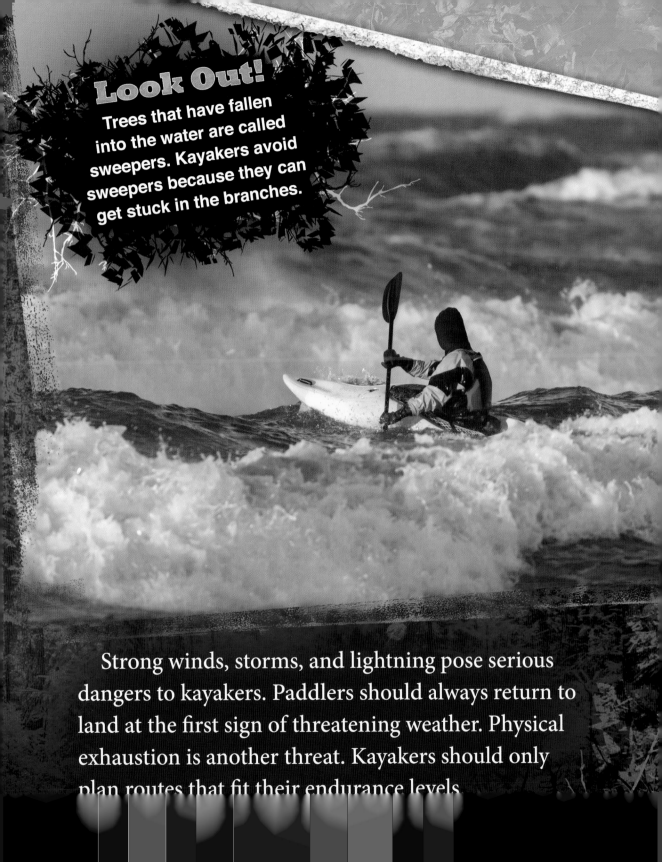

Look Out!

Trees that have fallen into the water are called sweepers. Kayakers avoid sweepers because they can get stuck in the branches.

Strong winds, storms, and lightning pose serious dangers to kayakers. Paddlers should always return to land at the first sign of threatening weather. Physical exhaustion is another threat. Kayakers should only plan routes that fit their endurance levels.

Many people live near a body of water where they can kayak. The easiest way to learn basic paddling and safety skills is to take lessons from a kayaking instructor. Many communities have paddling clubs. Members paddle together for recreation. They usually know the best places to kayak and enjoy teaching beginners.

Some kayakers prefer a lazy float on a lake. Others enjoy a challenging run through the rapids. Either way, kayaking is a great way to have fun and explore the outdoors.

Cleanup Crew

Paddling clubs often plan cleanup days. Kayakers pick up trash in the water and along the shores.

SEA KAYAKING IN ALASKA

Some of the best places to go sea kayaking are in Alaska. There, kayakers explore **bays** and **sounds** surrounded by spectacular scenery. Prince William Sound and Resurrection Bay are popular destinations. Kayakers paddle past **glaciers** and waterfalls while eagles soar overhead. Humpback whales, orcas, and porpoises break through the waves. Harbor seals sun themselves on rocks and swim in the water. Many kayakers join guided tours that last several hours. Some participate in multi-day kayak camping trips. No matter what type of trip they choose, kayakers are sure to have an Alaskan adventure they will never forget!

Alaska

N
W E
S

Resurrection
Bay

Prince William
Sound

Prince William Sound

GLOSSARY

bays—bodies of water partly enclosed by land

cockpits—large holes in kayaks where kayakers sit

deck—the top of a boat

dry suits—close-fitting waterproof suits that keep the body warm in cold water

eddy—a current of water that moves in a circular motion

endurance—the ability to do something for a long time

feathered—having one blade that is tilted at an angle

glaciers—massive sheets of ice that cover a large area of land

hulls—the sides and bottoms of boats

marshes—wetlands with a lot of plant growth

recreational—done for enjoyment

rudders—flat pieces of metal or wood mounted to the backs of boats for steering

sounds—large ocean inlets

spray skirt—a waterproof cover for the cockpit that stops water from getting into the kayak

whitewater—rough, fast-moving water

TO LEARN MORE

At the Library

De Medeiros, James. *Kayaking*. New York, N.Y.: Weigl
Publishers, 2008.

Mason, Paul. *Kayaking and Canoeing: The World's Best Paddling
Locations and Techniques*. Mankato, Minn.: Capstone Press, 2011.

Wurdinger, Scott, and Leslie Rapparlie. *Kayaking*. Mankato, Minn.:
Creative Education, 2007.

On the Web

Learning more about kayaking is
as easy as 1, 2, 3.

1. Go to www.factsurfer.com.

2. Enter "kayaking" into the search box.

3. Click the "Surf" button and you will see a list
of related Web sites.

With factsurfer.com, finding more information
is just a click away.

INDEX